THE HOME FRONT

BY TAMMY ZAMBO

Editorial Offices: Glenview, Illinois • Parsippany, New Jersey • New York, New York

Sales Offices: Needham, Massachusetts • Duluth, Georgia • Glenview, Illinois
Coppell, Texas • Sacramento, California • Mesa, Arizona

The Home Front

World War II was an armed conflict between the Allies and the Axis powers. In the United States, people focused on the progress of the war and on the troops who were fighting it. However, the United States could not have contributed to ending the war so successfully without the government, businesses, and millions of everyday people on the home front. People of all ages and from all parts of the country pulled together and made sacrifices for the war effort.

Women in the Military

After the bombing of Pearl Harbor, Hawaii, on December 7, 1941, the military needed to train millions of people for battle overseas. Many Americans eagerly volunteered. Others were required to serve because of the draft. All of these people, however, were men. Women were not allowed to serve on the battlefield and were not drafted.

Women pilots in the Women Airforce Service Pilots (WASP) flew many types of planes during the war.

The military had a problem, though. With a large number of men serving overseas, many important military positions on the home front were vacant. The military created units in which women could sign up to fill the empty positions.

In large numbers, women across the country signed up. They were proud to serve in the military, and were also determined to show everyone that they could do the jobs just as well as men.

Every branch of the military set up at least one organization specifically for women. Women in the army and navy nurse corps traveled all over the world to nurse wounded American soldiers and sailors. Women pilots who joined the Women Airforce Service Pilots (WASP) flew all types of planes, including fighters and bombers. One of their jobs was to deliver planes from factories to American troops who were waiting to take the planes overseas. Women in the Coast Guard Women's Reserve (known as SPARS) prepared parachutes and coded and decoded messages sent to ships. By the end of the war, more than 244,000 women had served in the military.

The Women in Military Service for America Memorial

The Women in Military Service for America Memorial in Arlington, Virginia, honors the nearly 2 million women who served in the military in World War II, in other United States wars, and in times of peace. Located at the entrance to Arlington National Cemetery, the memorial was dedicated and opened to the public in 1997. The memorial is really a small museum. It contains many artifacts, letters, and photographs pertaining to the role of women in the United States military.

Civilian Defense for All

Not everyone could serve in the military, but there were plenty of other necessary roles to fill. A new agency called the Office of Civilian Defense (OCD) encouraged citizens to give "an hour a day for the U.S.A." Towns and cities needed to be prepared in case they were attacked by an enemy, especially from the air. Some people volunteered to be wardens, organizing a block or a neighborhood to plan for air raids, or enemy aircraft attacks. They conducted alarm drills and made sure that people observed **blackouts**. A blackout is when lights are turned off to hide targets from the enemy during an air raid at night. Blackouts were also ordered along the East Coast so that American ships sailing close to shore would not be seen against city lights. This practice would keep ships more safe from attack by German submarines.

Many citizens who could fly planes volunteered for the Civil Air Patrol (CAP). CAP pilots flew small planes as they transported military staff, blood supplies, and mail from one place to another. They also flew over factories in mock bombing raids. They would drop sacks filled with flour to show that some landmarks needed to be disguised.

Aircraft and other war materials were built on assembly lines, just as cars had been during peacetime.

The Conversion of Business

All across the country, factories made adjustments to manufacture equipment, weapons, and other goods for the war. Automobile factories stopped making cars and started making trucks, tanks, and other military vehicles, as well as airplanes, engines, and many kinds of weapons. Aircraft parts were being made by a washing machine company. A producer of typewriters now manufactured rifles.

These changes to war production created millions of new jobs. These jobs paid better wages than many people could make in their hometowns, so over 15 million people moved. The United States had never before experienced so many people moving at once. Therefore, many cities experienced a severe shortage of housing.

Boomtowns

The population boomed in towns where shipyards, aircraft factories, and military bases were located. For this reason, they were called boomtowns. People moved to boomtowns so quickly that housing was scarce. Homeowners took in boarders, which meant that they rented spare rooms in their homes to strangers. Trailer and tent camps sprang up around many cities when space in houses ran out. Some people even slept in parked cars.

The community of Willow Run, Michigan, experienced rapid population growth when a new aircraft factory operated there. Eventually this factory would employ more than forty thousand people. To house its giant assembly line, the factory at Willow Run was one mile long! Another aircraft factory at Fort Worth, Texas, was so large that supervisors rode bicycles inside the building in order to visit different parts of the factory.

Even though millions of people endured hardships like these to find work during the war, most were thrilled with the result. Workers were paid well, and many people experienced opportunities they had never dreamed of. The Great Depression had finally ended.

Overcrowded boardinghouses were common in boomtowns. Here, factory workers are eating a meal.

The Boom is Nationwide

Shipyards along the east and west coasts of the United States were expanded during the war, and new shipyards were built. However, there was still a great need for more ships. Many ships that were used by the United States Navy during World War II were actually built on the Great Lakes in the midwestern United States! After they were completed, these ships were placed on large barges and floated down the Mississippi River to the ocean at New Orleans, Louisiana.

Many shipyards and factories operated twenty-four hours per day during the war. This meant that there were different shifts of workers who were busy each day. With so many workers crowding into the available housing in boomtowns, workers often had to take turns sleeping because there were not enough beds to go around. Often, a worker who had just finished working the daytime shift at a factory or a shipyard would go to sleep in a bed that had just been vacated by another worker who was leaving to work the evening shift.

Opportunities for Women

Those who found the greatest employment opportunities were women. Before the war, it was considered ideal for women to work in the home. However, millions of men had left their jobs to serve overseas, and millions of new jobs had been created. Women's skills were desperately needed for war work.

The government encouraged women to join the workforce, and more than six million of them did. Many of them were inspired by billboards and posters featuring images such as Rosie the Riveter. They were eager to contribute to the war effort, and they tackled their new jobs with enthusiasm.

Still, many men did not believe women could perform factory jobs as well as men. They sometimes teased and joked about the women workers. Often their comments only encouraged women to show the men—and themselves—that they were fully able to do their jobs.

This poster of Rosie the Riveter, and others like it, urged women to go to work for the war effort.

Besides the women who worked for wages, millions of women worked in important programs as volunteers. In the Red Cross, they operated snack bars called canteens, served as nurses' aides, and drove ambulances. They also worked in civilian defense programs and at USO (United Service Organizations) centers. These centers provided entertainment for soldiers.

By 1944, 36 percent of the paid workforce was made up of women. Without their contributions, the Allies could not have won the war. Yet women were paid 40 percent less than men for working in the same jobs. In addition, most women lost their jobs to men when the men came home from war. Many women returned to homemaking, even though they preferred to keep working outside the home.

Many women joined the workforce, as in this assembly line.

Japanese American families wait for a bus to take them to an internment camp. The children are wearing identification tags in case they become separated from their parents.

The Internment Camps

Americans pulled together to win the war, and their determination boosted their spirits. For many people, however, pulling together also meant discriminating against some of their fellow Americans. After Japan bombed the United States naval base at Pearl Harbor, many people felt that Japanese Americans could not be trusted. They were afraid that some Japanese Americans might give important information to the Japanese government or damage property in the United States. The government also had the same fears about Japanese Americans.

Immigrants from Japan could not yet become United States citizens, but they were loyal to America anyway. In addition, their children who were born in the United States automatically became citizens. Nevertheless, in February 1942, President Franklin Roosevelt signed an order which allowed United States Army commanders to order the removal of Japanese Americans from the West Coast of the United States.

Shortly thereafter, some 120,000 Japanese Americans had to leave or sell their homes and businesses, or trust others to keep them safe until they could return. The Japanese Americans were taken to **internment** camps built especially to house them. Eight of the ten camps were located in isolated and barren areas in six western states. Two more were located in Arkansas. Surrounded by barbed wire and guarded by soldiers, the Japanese Americans were forced to live in the cramped, dusty camps. Once there, they tried to reestablish a normal daily life.

Despite the harsh way they were treated, Japanese Americans were very patriotic. Many Japanese American men served in the United States Army during the war. Japanese Americans were forced to stay in the camps for as long as three years. Gradually, however, the government released them. Finally, in early 1945, the camps began to close.

Japanese Americans lived in assembly centers while the relocation centers (internment camps) were being built.

Daily Life on the Home Front

Every day Americans were reminded of the war. The most constant reminders were shortages and **rationing**. Many ordinary goods were scarce. Metal was needed for building ships, airplanes, vehicles, and weapons, so items like bicycles were not produced. Automobile factories were used for war production, so new cars for private citizens were not built. Supplies of shoes were limited because the leather was needed for soldiers' boots.

Common foods such as sugar, coffee, butter, cheese, and meat were rationed so that everyone got some but no one got too much. Every family was given ration books with stamps that represented points used to buy certain products.

To help feed their families, many people all over the country grew their own vegetables in victory gardens. These gardens became so popular that they produced more than one-third of the vegetables eaten in the United States during the war. Households gave away any extra vegetables to the needy, or canned them for later use.

Gasoline was also rationed, and Americans adopted new habits to get from place to place. Walking and carpooling became common. For longer journeys, people took trains. Frequently, though, they did not go anywhere at all. Families stayed at home. Many adults were working extra hours in factories and did not have much time to travel anyway.

The banner shows how many family members are serving in the military.

People also wrote letters often, especially if a family member was in the military. Families hung a banner in the window, with blue stars to show how many members of the family were serving in the military. If one of them died, the blue star would be replaced with a gold one.

Children responded gladly when President Roosevelt asked the nation to recycle scrap rubber and metal.

Children on the Home Front

Children played important roles in the war effort. Many of them joined civilian defense teams. One boy in New York, for example, was an air raid messenger. He passed on messages between commanders at air raid posts during alarm drills.

Children organized scrap drives, collecting paper, metal cans, and rubber tires from people in their neighborhood. They also contributed their own metal toys and foil that they had saved from packages of gum. These items were recycled to make war-related goods.

In their spare time, children listened to radio programs such as *The Lone Ranger* and *The Shadow*. They read comic books featuring Captain Marvel, Batman, and Superman. Newspaper comics such as *Little Orphan Annie* were popular too. Going to the movies was a regular weekend event for many families. For about ten cents, each person could watch a double feature, or two movies. Between the two movies, newsreels, or news reports, updated them with images of the war.

Many teenagers worked in factories and on farms. Many states eased child-labor laws during the war so that teenagers could work. Nearly three million girls and boys were working by 1943.

In their spare time, teenagers enjoyed listening to swing music played by "big bands" led by Glen Miller, Benny Goodman, Duke Ellington, and others. A young singer, Frank Sinatra, was hugely popular. In 1944, thousands of teenage girls nearly rioted as they tried to get near him.

What Mattered Most

Millions of Americans worked hard and made many sacrifices on the home front in World War II. Daily life for nearly everyone changed completely. However, even though life was not easy, people found comfort in the thought that they were helping men and women who were serving in the military. They thought their efforts were helping to win the war, which was what mattered most.

Glossary

blackout turning out of lights to hide targets from an enemy during an air raid at night and from submarines offshore

internment holding and limiting the movement of people during wartime

rationing government limiting the amount of food and other goods each person can buy